Lake Oswego Jr. High
2500 Country Club Rd.
Lake Oswego, OR 97034
503-534-2335

Queens and Princesses

PRINCESS

Grace

OF MONACO

by Tim O'Shei

Consultant:

Glenn Steinberg, PhD

Associate Professor of English

The College of New Jersey

Ewing, New Jersey

Capstone press®

Mankato, Minnesota

Snap Books are published by Capstone Press,
151 Good Counsel Drive, P.O. Box 669, Mankato, Minnesota 56002.
www.capstonepress.com

Library of Congress Cataloging-in-Publication Data
O'Shei, Tim.
    Princess Grace of Monaco / by Tim O'Shei.
    p. cm. — (Snap books. Queens and princesses)
    Summary: "Describes the life and death of Princess Grace of Monaco" — Provided
by publisher.
    Includes bibliographical references and index.
    ISBN-13: 978-1-4296-1957-8 (hardcover)
    ISBN-10: 1-4296-1957-0 (hardcover)
    1. Grace, Princess of Monaco, 1929–1982 — Juvenile literature. 2. Princesses —
Monaco — Biography — Juvenile literature. 3. Motion picture actors and actresses
— United States — Biography — Juvenile literature. I. Title. II. Series.
DC943.G7O74 2009
944.9'49092 — dc22   2008007551

Editor: Angie Kaelberer
Designer: Juliette Peters
Photo Researcher: Wanda Winch

Photo Credits: Alamy/Pictorial Press Ltd., cover, 17; AP Images, 19, 25, 29;
Corbis/Bettmann, 5, 23; Getty Images Inc./Anwar Hussein, 26; Getty Images Inc./
Hulton Archive/Evening Standard, 11; Getty Images Inc./Hulton Archive/Silver
Screen Collection, 15; Getty Images Inc./Time Life Pictures/Frank Scherschel, 6;
Getty Images Inc./Time Life Pictures /Sharland, 21; Getty Images Inc./WireImage/
Anwar Hussein, 28; The Image Works/Roger-Viollet, 14; The Image Works/SSPL/
Manchester Daily Express, 24; Shutterstock/Mirec, 7; Temple University Libraries,
Urban Archives, Philadelphia, PA, 9, 13

Essential content terms are **bold** and are defined at the bottom of the page where
they first appear.

1 2 3 4 5 6 13 12 11 10 09 08

30092000142847

Table of Contents

FROM *Star* TO *Princess*

In April 1956, Grace Kelly was only 26, but she was already famous. She was a movie star, an Oscar winner, and one of the most photographed women in the world.

Grace had just finished filming her last movie, *High Society*. On April 4, 20 relatives and 50 friends joined her aboard the ocean liner *Constitution*. They were headed from New York City to a small European country called Monaco. There, Grace's life would change forever.

Grace Kelly (front row, center), her father (left), and her mother (right), traveled to Monaco on an ocean liner.

Grace's family and friends weren't the only passengers. About 100 news reporters and photographers also bought tickets. They recorded Grace's every move. To get some privacy, Grace spent a lot of time in her cabin. She wrote letters to friends and worked on knitting.

Though she tried to hide it, Grace was nervous. "What's going to happen to me?" she wondered. "What would this new life be like?"

Prince Rainier (right) followed Grace (center) off the yacht to Monaco's shore.

Soon, Grace had her answer. On April 12, eight days after leaving New York, *Constitution* reached Monaco. The ship was so large that it couldn't dock at the shore. Instead, the man who had been waiting for Grace sailed out to meet her on his **yacht**. A plank was extended from the ship to the yacht. Wearing a large white hat and a navy blue coat, Grace carefully walked across the plank. The thousands of people who crowded in the harbor and on rooftops watched closely. A plane overhead dropped red and white flowers across the harbor.

Grace reached the yacht. The man, Prince Rainier III, held out his hand to her. She took it. Grace was about to become the prince's wife. When she did, she would no longer be simply Grace Kelly. She would be known as Her Serene Highness Princess Grace of Monaco.

A TINY LAND

Monaco is a principality, or a small, independent land that is ruled by a prince. Prince Rainier III's family, the Grimaldis, have ruled Monaco for almost 700 years.

Monaco is located in western Europe on the Mediterranean Sea. It covers only .76 square miles (2 square kilometers). That's a little more than half the size of Central Park in New York City. Monaco has about 32,000 residents. The weather is warm year-round, which makes it an attractive vacation spot.

yacht — a large boat used for sailing or racing

AN AMERICAN
Childhood

Grace Patricia Kelly was born in Philadelphia, Pennsylvania, on November 12, 1929. She grew up with two older siblings, Peggy and Jack Jr. She also had a younger sister, Lizanne.

The Kelly family was talented. Their mother, Margaret, was a former physical education teacher and swim coach. Their father, Jack, was a star athlete. He earned an Olympic gold medal in a type of boat racing called sculling. Later, he started a bricklaying business that made him a millionaire.

Grace's uncles were well known in show business. Walter Kelly was a **vaudeville** comedian who traveled the world making people laugh. George Kelly was a famous playwright. Having uncles in the entertainment field helped Grace decide to pursue it herself.

Grace (center) grew up with sisters Peggy and Lizanne (left) and brother Jack (right).

vaudeville — a stage show that may include comedy, music, magic, and stunts

SHY BUT TOUGH

Grace's sisters and brother were all outgoing and athletic. Grace was different. As a child, she was shy and often sick with colds and allergies. She preferred quieter activities. She loved to read stories. She used her dolls to put on make-believe stage shows. She took dance lessons and dreamed of becoming a **ballerina**.

But Grace also had a temper. It exploded one day when her brother and his friends had a tomato fight with another group of boys. Grace got caught in the crossfire, and a tomato squashed her in the face. She started fighting back. She didn't stop until one of her family's household helpers broke up the fight.

FAMOUS FUTURE

In high school, Grace was one of the most popular girls in her class. Boys liked her, and Grace dated often. But if her father didn't think the boy was good enough for her, Grace usually broke off the relationship. Jack didn't like many of Grace's boyfriends. As a result, Grace broke many hearts.

Grace still loved to dance, but she was 5 feet, 7 inches (1.7 meters) tall. That was too tall to be a ballerina. Instead, Grace focused her love of performing on the theater. She acted in her first play at age 12. In high school, she won leading roles in school plays. Her high school yearbook had this prediction: "Miss Grace P. Kelly, a famous star of stage and screen."

ballerina — a female ballet dancer

> "I was rather shy — certainly never much of an extrovert. They were wonderful years and terrible years. Anxious years. Not very happy."
>
> Grace, speaking about her years in high school

Unlike her brother, Jack, and sister Peggy, Grace (center) wasn't a star athlete.

Grace

THE STAR

Grace planned to study dance at Bennington College in Vermont. But the school turned her down because her math scores were too low. She wasn't too disappointed, though. Grace really wanted a career in theater. A family friend helped her get an **audition** at the American Academy of Dramatic Arts in New York City. The school was full, but Grace's connection to playwright George Kelly helped her get accepted.

Grace moved to New York City in 1947 to attend the American Academy of Dramatic Arts.

audition — a tryout performance for an actor or actress

BECOMING AN ACTRESS

Grace moved to New York and spent the next two years in school. She attended classes in the morning and earned money by modeling in the afternoon.

After graduating in 1949, Grace tried out for roles in Broadway plays. She landed a part in a play called *The Father*. The play closed after a couple of months, but Grace's performance earned good reviews. That job didn't lead to more, though. For the next two years, Grace auditioned for parts in more than 40 Broadway plays. She didn't get any of them.

In 1955, Grace starred in *To Catch a Thief* with famous actor Cary Grant.

In 1955, Grace won the highest award in film acting, the Oscar.

Grace had better luck in television, which was just becoming popular. During her first three years as a professional actress, Grace appeared on 60 TV shows. They included episodes of *Hallmark Television Playhouse* and *Studio One*. That success led to movie opportunities in Hollywood. The first came in 1951 when Grace won a part in the movie *Fourteen Hours*. Her second movie, at age 22, is one of her most memorable. Grace starred in a western movie called *High Noon*. For another movie, *Mogambo*, Grace traveled to Africa.

By 1954, Grace was a major star. Her talent caught the attention of director Alfred Hitchcock, who was famous for his suspense movies. She starred in three of his movies, *Dial M for Murder*, *Rear Window*, and *To Catch a Thief*. In 1955, she won the Best Actress Oscar for her performance as a suspicious wife in *The Country Girl*.

MEETING THE PRINCE

By 1955, Grace was one of the world's most popular movie stars. She received many requests for photo shoots. In May 1955, Grace was in Cannes, France, for a film festival. The magazine *Paris Match* set up a shoot with her and Prince Rainier III of nearby Monaco.

The morning of the shoot, nothing went right for Grace. When she plugged in her hair dryer, the electricity was off. That meant that she couldn't iron the dress she had planned to wear. She slicked her wet hair back in a bun and put on the least-wrinkled dress in her suitcase. She hated the dress, but she figured few people would ever see the pictures.

During the short drive from Cannes to Monaco, Grace was slightly nervous. She wasn't sure what the prince would be like or even what to call him. But when they met, the two connected quickly. Prince Rainier gave Grace a tour of his flower garden and his personal zoo. Wanting to impress her, Rainier stuck his hand into a tiger cage and petted the big cat.

It worked. On the ride back, Grace told her companions that she liked the prince. "He is charming," she said. "So very charming."

A PRINCELY PEN PAL

When Grace was a little girl, her mother taught her to send thank-you notes. Right away, Grace sent one to Prince Rainier. He was happy to hear from her and wrote back. During that summer and fall, they secretly exchanged letters. In December, the prince surprised Grace by showing up in Philadelphia. She was even more charmed than before.

Rainier met Grace's family at a Christmas party. Her parents liked him too. They were pleased that he was a Catholic, like the Kellys. By New Year's Eve, Grace and Rainier were engaged. They planned their wedding for four months later.

Before her wedding, Grace made her last movie, *High Society*. In the movie, Grace wore the dazzling 11-carat diamond engagement ring Prince Rainier gave her.

Grace started planning her wedding while she was filming. The movie's costume designer, Helen Rose, created her wedding gown. It was made of ivory silk taffeta and decorated with pearls and 450 yards (411 meters) of lace. About 30 people worked on the gown, which took six weeks to make.

Grace showed off her engagement ring to her mother, Margaret (left), Rainier, and her father, Jack (right).

CELEBRATING
Grace

When Grace arrived for the April 1956 wedding, all of Monaco celebrated. Banners with the letters "R" and "G" hung in the streets. Schoolchildren wrote poems for Grace. People danced in the streets. Fireworks lit the sky.

The wedding celebration lasted two days. On April 18, Rainier and Grace were legally married in a small ceremony. Grace wore a beige lace-and-taffeta suit and a matching hat. The prince and princess held a religious wedding the next day. Six hundred people packed into St. Nicholas Cathedral for the ceremony. Another 30 million around the world watched on TV.

Grace and Rainier's church wedding took place on April 19, 1956.

UPLANDS ELEMENTARY
LAKE OSWEGO, OR

Fragrant white lilies, hydrangeas, and lilacs decorated the church. Grace glowed in her elegant gown. She carried a bouquet of lilies-of-the-valley and a small Bible. For good luck, she stuck a penny in her left shoe. Grace's matron of honor was her sister Peggy. Peggy and the six bridesmaids wore hats and flowing yellow dresses. The four flower girls wore white dresses and flowered tiaras.

Grace's former movie studio, MGM, captured the events on film. Grace had a contract to make several more movies for MGM. But as a princess, she wasn't allowed to make movies. The MGM bosses agreed to drop the contract. In return, Grace allowed them to film the ceremony. MGM made it into a movie called *The Wedding of the Century*.

SWEET BEGINNINGS

After the church wedding, a **reception** was held in the palace courtyard. The gifts were fitting for royalty. They included a yacht, diamond jewelry, and a Rolls-Royce convertible from the people of Monaco.

The wedding cake was equally elegant. It had six levels. Each level was decorated with sugar figurines that showed scenes from Monaco's history. On the bottom level was a sugar model of the palace.

Prince Rainier used his sword to make a first slice into the cake. It was a sweet beginning to a marriage that would be remembered forever.

reception — a formal party

A STYLE TRENDSETTER

Grace was known for her sense of style. She always looked elegant, whether she was dancing at a formal ball or relaxing in Capri pants and sunglasses.

Right after Grace's wedding, dressmakers began copying the design of her wedding gown. They figured that if the dress was elegant enough for Grace, other brides would want to wear it too.

Six months later, Grace returned to the United States for a visit. She was pregnant but wanted to keep it secret. She used a crocodile-skin Hermès handbag to cover her stomach. The bag became known as the Kelly bag. Even today, there is a one-year waiting list to buy that bag.

GRACE
OF MONACO

At first, Grace's life as a princess was gloomy. Monaco is so small that there wasn't much to do. Rainier was busy running the country, but Grace was hardly ever alone. The palace servants and security guards were always nearby and watching. Grace was homesick and felt like she had lost her freedom.

Still, Grace was committed to making life as a princess work. She asked her family to send packages of American goods. Boxes arrived packed with everything from toilet paper to dog biscuits to cake mixes.

The palace had more than 200 rooms, but many of them were outdated. Grace brightened the palace with flowers and furniture. She learned to speak French, which is Monaco's main language.

Grace was homesick and lonely during the early days of her marriage.

In 1958, Grace took over the leadership of Monaco's Red Cross. Every summer, she hosted the Red Cross Ball to raise money for the organization. She invited her Hollywood friends, which attracted more people to the event.

Eventually, Grace began to feel at home. She was especially fond of Monaco's children. She helped open a day-care center. She also regularly visited Monaco's orphanage. Every Christmas, she brought gifts to the children there.

Grace was also proud of her Irish heritage. She collected books by Irish authors and sheet music of Irish songs. Today, her collection is open to the public in the Princess Grace Irish Library in Monaco.

Grace proudly wore her Red Cross honorary medal in 1959. She led Monaco's chapter of the Red Cross for many years.

Grace and Rainier had three children, Albert (left), Stephanie (on Grace's lap), and Caroline (right).

A ROYAL FAMILY

Of all the jobs that Princess Grace had, being a mother was her favorite. The prince and princess had three children. Caroline was born in 1957. Albert, who would become Monaco's ruler in 2005, was born one year later. Their third child, Stephanie, came in 1965.

Grace was very involved with her children. The kids especially enjoyed when their mother read stories like *Alice in Wonderland* aloud to them. Her years as an actress made her very good at acting out the fairy-tale voices.

LOVE OF PERFORMING

Grace missed acting and hoped one day to do it again. In 1962, Alfred Hitchcock offered Grace the lead in his movie *Marnie*. The part called for her to play a thief and kiss actor Sean Connery. Rainier told Grace that she could do it, but the people of Monaco wouldn't have it. They didn't want to see their princess kissing another man. Grace followed her people's wishes. She turned down the part.

Grace's movie career was over. But she still found ways to continue her love of performing. She helped build a theater and a dance school in Monaco. She also appeared in TV documentaries about Monaco. In 1976, Grace started performing at poetry recitals all over the world. Audiences enjoyed listening to her soft, clear voice as she recited poems.

In 1979, Princess Grace recited poems at a poetry reading in Edinburgh, Scotland.

> "One doesn't feel older until you start getting aches and pains and have to curtail or adjust your activities. That hasn't happened to me — yet. I'm lucky and am just looking forward to what comes next."
>
> Princess Grace, 1982

A TRAGIC ACCIDENT

On September 13, 1982, Grace was driving on a winding Monaco road with her 17-year-old daughter, Stephanie. Suddenly, Grace lost control of the car. It veered off the road and plunged down a 120-foot (37-meter) cliff.

Stephanie was injured but alive. Her mother wasn't so lucky. Doctors believed that Grace most likely had a **stroke** while driving. The stroke caused her to lose control of the car. Grace's head injuries were so serious that she went into a coma. Grace died the next day. The world had lost its movie star princess.

Prince Rainier lived another 23 years, but sadness always cast a shadow on his heart. He was asked once if he would ever consider getting married again. His answer was no. "How could I?" he said. "Everywhere I go, I see Grace."

stroke — when a blocked blood vessel prevents oxygen from reaching the brain

Princess Grace (left) and Lady Diana Spencer (right) in 1981.

A PRINCESS' ADVICE

In March 1981, Princess Grace met Lady Diana Spencer at a party in London, England. Diana had just become engaged to Charles, the Prince of Wales and future king of England. She was getting a huge amount of attention. Photographers followed her everywhere. Reporters wrote about everything she did or said.

Princess Grace pulled Diana aside. Diana asked her what life would really be like as a princess. "It gets worse!" Grace said, but she gave the answer with a hug. That hug was a silent way of letting Diana know that she would also learn to handle the spotlight. And she did. When Grace died the next year, Diana took over as the world's most graceful princess.

GRACE'S LEGACY

The rest of the world still sees Grace, too, because her work is still alive. A hospital she opened in London, England, in 1977 still serves patients. Her interest in the arts lives on too. Soon after Grace's death, Rainier started the Princess Grace Foundation-USA. This organization gives money to people who want to work in theater, film, or dance.

In life, Grace Kelly was a master of the stage — first in theater, then on film, and finally for Monaco. No matter what stage she was on, she performed with style and, of course, with grace.

People still remember Princess Grace for her beauty, kindness, and style.

Glossary

audition (aw-DISH-uhn) — a tryout performance for an actor

ballerina (bal-uh-REE-nuh) — a female ballet dancer

coma (KOH-muh) — a medical condition in which a person is unconscious, or in a deep state of sleep, for a long period of time

contract (KAHN-trakt) — a legal agreement between people stating the terms by which one will work for the other

principality (prin-suh-PA-luh-tee) — a land ruled by a prince

reception (ri-SEP-shuhn) — a formal party; receptions are often held after weddings.

role (ROHL) — an actor's part in a movie or play

stroke (STROHK) — a medical condition that occurs when a blocked blood vessel stops oxygen from reaching the brain

vaudeville (VOD-vill) — a stage show that may include comedy, music, magic, and stunts

yacht (YAHT) — a large boat used for sailing or racing

Read More

Gallagher, Debbie. *Palaces, Mansions, and Castles.* Homes around the World. North Mankato, Minn.: Smart Apple Media, 2007.

King, David C. *Monaco.* Cultures of the World. New York: Marshall Cavendish Benchmark, 2008.

Roshell, Starshine. *Real-Life Royalty.* Reading Rocks! Mankato, Minn.: Child's World, 2008.

Internet Sites

FactHound offers a safe, fun way to find Internet sites related to this book. All of the sites on FactHound have been researched by our staff.

Here's how:

1. Visit *www.facthound.com*
2. Choose your grade level.
3. Type in this book ID **1429619570** for age-appropriate sites. You may also browse subjects by clicking on letters, or by clicking on pictures and words.
4. Click on the **Fetch It** button.

FactHound will fetch the best sites for you!

Index